# Angels Among Us

## A Collection of Inspiring True Angel Stories

# E. Lonnie Melashenko
# with Brian Jones

**Pacific Press® Publishing Association**
Nampa, Idaho
Oshawa, Ontario, Canada

Edited by B. Russell Holt
Designed by Dennis Ferree
Inside art: page 13, Clyde Provonsha; 18, Norman Brice; 24, C. Block;
33, Lars Justinen; 42, P. J. Rennings; 51, Lars Justinen; 54, Helen Tarrey;
56, Lars Justinen; 60, John Lear; 64, Lars Justinen; 78, Norman Brice;
82, John Lear; 84 Norman Brice.

ISBN 0-8163-1792-5

# Contents

# Introduction

Have you ever wondered, "Why all the interest in angels today?" Stories abound about people's experiences with angels. Often it doesn't seem to matter if those who have these experiences are at all spiritual or if their lives change significantly as a result of their encounter with angels. We're almost at the point where it's become embarrassing to be without one's own personal angel story. "You mean, you haven't seen an angel yet? What's the matter with you?"

But the "un-angeled" who have missed meeting one of these celestial celebrities may take comfort in buying angel T-shirts, angel figurines, angel chocolates, angel calendars, angel necklaces, angel dolls, angel stationery, angel cards—and angel books. Or they may watch TV programs, such as *Touched by an Angel.* Has the whole subject become commercialized and trivialized? Has the popularity of angels so saturated the market and airwaves that we have become glutted with the subject and are ready to turn to some new fad?

The authors of this book think that from the perspective of God's Word, most people in our culture have been given a distorted and misleading view of angels. Clouds of hype, trivia, and fantasy surround this subject today that have as much relevance to the real meaning of angels as Easter bunnies have to do with the resurrection of Jesus.

Think about it from the standpoint of the Bible's last book, Revelation. In this book, the apostle John describes the wrap-up of human history leading up to Christ's Second Coming. Revelation is a short book. You can read it (if you don't stop very long to ponder its meaning) in about twenty minutes. But in this brief, fascinating account of things past, present, and future, you will find more than seventy-five references to angels! In Revelation you will find angels bearing messages to the whole world; angels holding back winds of war and strife; angels carrying out missions of divine judgment; angels engaged in cosmic war; angels traveling at quantum speeds between heaven and earth; angels singing songs of praise; angels giving glory to God; and angels refusing worship.

This book proposes to answer some questions about angels. Who are they? What is their connection with humanity? What are their main activities? Are there evil angels as well as good ones? How can you tell the difference? Do I have a guardian angel? Can I communicate with him? What part will angels play in my future? What part do they play in my life now?

It is the aim of this book to answer these questions and others just as important to you. We offer these answers from God's Word in the setting of some of the most amazing true angel stories that have taken place in the history of the world, from Bible times to our day. So, prepare yourself as we take off on a flight to realms far more amazing, relevant, and real than any that science-fiction writers and fable-makers have imagined in their most dazzling dreams and daring moments.

# The Man Who Couldn't Be Killed

Does God still send angels to protect His people as He did in Bible times? During a revolutionary period a few years ago in an African country that is still in political turmoil, Mike Pearson served as pastor in a large district situated in the midst of the conflict. Three times a week he had to drive on a main highway where the traffic was sparse because of guerrilla activity. Anybody who traveled that way was subject to being killed without cause. But Pastor Mike was faithful, and several times a week for about two years he drove along this road as he fulfilled his pastoral duties.

Finally the day came when the two sides declared a truce, and a shaky peace returned to that African country. One day Pastor Mike had some official business to conduct at a government office. After completing his errand, he came out of the building and was astonished to be greeted by a tall man in military dress, with bandoleers and grenades attached to his uniform. With a genial smile the soldier said to Pastor Pearson, "Sir, I'd like to shake your hand."

Pastor Mike is a friendly person, but this approach from such a stranger took him by surprise. So he answered, "Oh, why would you like to do that?"

The soldier replied, "I'd like to shake the hand of the man we could not kill."

Pastor Mike said, "Please explain."

"Did you not travel on the main highway every Monday, Wednesday, and Thursday and pass the midpoint at about 10:00 A.M. on those days in your brown Toyota wagon?"

"Yes," Pastor Mike answered, his curiosity rising.

"Well, sir, on seven different occasions my fellow guards and I tried to kill you. Our plan was to shoot you as you drove by. Each time you came along, we had you clearly in sight from our post in the bush, but our guns refused to work when we pressed the triggers. As soon as you drove out of our range, our guns would work again. We carefully tested our AK 47's before and after your passing through that way, and they worked flawlessly. But then they simply would not fire when we directed them at you. It could only have been a spirit or an angel that kept our guns from working. So, that's why I'd like to shake your hand. God is on your side—or you are on His!"

What a strange experience it must have been for Pastor Pearson to shake the hand of his would-be assassin! But how gratifying for him to know that he was under the care of angels even when he was oblivious of danger.

"He shall give His angels charge over you, to keep you in all your ways" (Psalm 91:11). Two opposite reasons have made this perhaps the most famous angel verse in the Bible. The first is that it comes from the 91st Psalm, which God's people have treasured for thousands of years. The second reason is that Satan tried to make deceptive use of this verse when tempting Jesus in the wilderness. He wanted the Savior to presume on God's protecting care by jumping off the pinnacle of the temple, and thereby challenge His Father to give Him a safe landing. Jesus would never allow Himself to be lured into "daring" God to prove His Word. Not only did Satan misapply this verse when presenting it to Jesus as an excuse for recklessly endangering His life, but he also misquoted it. Satan omitted the words "in all your ways." God will keep us safe and secure when *our ways* harmonize with *His* way.

# The Stranger in the Brown Overcoat

On a bitterly cold day in January 1940, the car taking the Thomas family into London crept along the slippery road. In spite of constant movement, the windshield wipers could not keep the windshield clear of the snow that was falling thick and fast. Several times Pastor Thomas stopped the car and brushed the snow away. It was nearly dark when the family finally reached the railway station where they would take the train to the channel port of Folkestone. From there they would cross to France.

The Thomas family had been home for a year from Kenya, in east Africa. During that fateful year, England and the empire had been plunged into the horrors of World War II. Although no bombs had yet fallen on Britain, many ships had been sunk in the waters surrounding the island. Because of the dangers of sea travel, the returning missionary family decided to go from France to Italy by train, then take a neutral ship to the east African port of Mombasa.

Pastor and Mrs. Thomas and their four sons, ranging in age from three to thirteen, stood in the pitch blackness of the railway station, holding onto their suitcases, and waiting for the train to come. The blackout was a serious matter in those days. Civil authorities allowed no lights of any kind that might be seen from the air.

The Thomas family heard, rather than saw, the coaches as they came to a stop in front of them. Tightly holding hands, the Thomases boarded the train. Five hundred soldiers also got on. The doors slammed, the guard blew his whistle, and the train slowly pulled out of the station.

How strange it felt to be riding along in the blackness of night! Conversations were going on all around them, but they could not see a single soul. Some of the soldiers were singing, some were cursing the war that had taken them from their homes and families. The minutes seemed to pass slowly as the rails clicked off the miles.

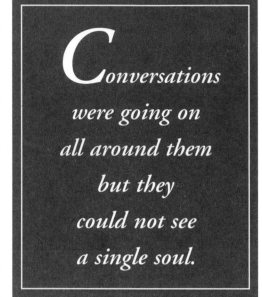

*Conversations were going on all around them but they could not see a single soul.*

Noses pressed against the window, the Thomas boys could see no friendly lights from farmhouses, nor from any of the villages they passed through. Even the ground, though covered with snow, could hardly be seen in the gloom. After what seemed like hours, the train began to slow down as it neared the seacoast where the steamer was waiting to take them across the English Channel to France.

Once again Pastor Thomas reminded the boys to keep together, hold hands, and follow him. The train stopped, and hundreds of passengers poured onto the platform, the Thomas family among them. But where were they to go? An icy wind blew around them as they stood, bewildered. Suddenly a tall man appeared out of the darkness.

"Follow me," he said. "I know where you must go."

Down the platform they followed his dimly visible form. He led them through a dark room into another that was well lighted. For a few minutes all they could do was blink, the lights seemed so bright. Then they saw that this was the room where officials would examine their passports and luggage. They turned to look at their guide and saw that he was a tall man dressed in a heavy brown overcoat.

The man led them to a table where an officer sat ready to inspect their passports. The officer asked whether Pastor Thomas was carrying any letters. During the war, military officials would very carefully inspect all letters leaving or entering England to see that they contained no important information that might help the enemy. Pastor Thomas admitted that he was carrying some letters, and at the request of the officer, he laid them on the table.

The letters had been written by former missionaries in Kenya, and Pastor Thomas was carrying them to African people whom the missionaries had known. They were all written in Luo, an African language. This was very serious indeed because, no one in that room could read and translate the letters except Pastor Thomas himself, and the officer said that he could not accept Pastor Thomas's word.

Just then the man in the brown coat spoke up. "These are missionaries," he said. "I know them, and I know that there is nothing in those letters dangerous to our country."

"Very well," said the officer, "we will let them pass."

Pastor Thomas looked at the stranger in surprise. Where had this man ever known the Thomas family? When had he read those letters? It was very mysterious. Pastor Thomas expressed his gratitude to him. The man did not answer but proceeded to help them out of another difficulty.

All over the room, customs officers were examining luggage. They were taking no chances. One of the officials came to Pastor Thomas and indicated that he wanted the luggage opened for inspection. Pastor Thomas had not expected this. Ordinarily, British subjects traveling in peacetime did not have their luggage inspected when going from one part of the empire to another. Knowing this, and not stopping to think of the difference wartime might make, he had strapped up his suitcases very thoroughly. The idea of opening them all now filled him with dismay.

The man in the brown coat spoke up again.

"These people are missionaries," he told the inspector. "I can vouch for their luggage. It does not contain anything prohibited by law."

"Very well," said the officer briskly, and motioned them toward the door leading to the gangplank.

A few minutes later the family had climbed aboard the ship. Dim lights burned here and there in the long corridors. One of the stewards came to meet them. He explained that the soldiers had taken almost all the beds on board, but he did have a few places for the ladies. He asked Mrs. Thomas to follow him.

Mrs. Thomas shook her head. "No, I am not going to be separated from my husband. If this ship is going to be torpedoed, the whole family will go down together." Seeing she was determined to stay with her husband and their boys, the steward shrugged his shoulders and went on his way.

Almost instinctively Pastor Thomas turned to the man in the brown coat. For the third time, he did not fail them.

"I know a place for you," he said. "It is not an ideal place for a missionary family to sleep, but at least you will not be disturbed."

He led them to the ship's bar. It was after midnight, and the bar was closed. Around the room by the walls were leather-padded benches. On these, the family could lie down and rest for the remainder of the night.

Pastor Thomas pushed the suitcases one by one under the benches. Then he turned to thank the tall stranger once more for all his kindness. But he was gone! Stepping quickly into the hall, Pastor Thomas looked up and down the passage. He could see no sign of the man. He went to the top of the gangplank and asked the officers there whether they had seen the man in the brown coat.

"There wasn't anyone like that on the boat tonight," they replied. "If there had been, we would have seen him."

Yet Pastor Thomas knew there had been such a man, for he had talked with him. But now he had disappeared into the night.

He returned to the barroom and reported to his family. "It must have been an angel," said Mrs. Thomas softly.—Adapted from *Only in Africa*, by Virgil E. Robinson (Review and Herald, 1965), pp. 97-101.

CHAPTER
3

# A Tall
# American Angel

Nick and Claudia Parks, a couple from Lincoln, Nebraska, signed up to serve as English teachers in a city in northern China. During their first tour of duty they taught at the provincial university and lived in a "Foreign Expert Building," where they could be kept under the ever-watchful eyes of officialdom. Between university students in the daytime and government workers in the evening, Nick and Claudia taught about 500 students each week. In this city of six million, there are fewer than fifty Americans at any one time.

On Thanksgiving Day, 1993, Nick and Claudia were scheduled to start class with a new group of students. The classroom assigned for their use was cold and bleak. Sharp Siberian winds knifed through the loosely hinged windows to kill whatever warmth might accumulate from the people gathered in the room. Claudia tells the rest of the story in her own words:

In class, after enrolling and designating English names to this diverse group, I decided to tell a story and test our students' listening comprehension. I told them the story of Pollyanna. They loved the idea of learning to play the "Glad Game" and to hunt for something in every situation to be glad about. We were glad that putting smiles on our faces, even here in China, could melt frozen hearts and smooth the way for us to make forever friends.

"Dear Jesus," I prayed, "please give us a sign that You're in this place and that You still care for us."

For the last half of our class we had "free talk." The students really like that time. We divided the class into two sections. I moved my group to the top part of the room. The students circled closely around each of us so we could talk and listen together. Below and to my left I could hear them asking Nick questions about his Christianity and if he really believed and accepted Jesus as his personal Savior. I was proud of him for speaking boldly about his faith even though he recognized the danger. This is not America. Religious freedom is different here from the way it is in our homeland. But questions of the heart need to be answered.

My group talked about other things. They asked me to sing for them, so I taught them *Over the River and Through the Woods* and *Jesus Loves the Little Children, All the Children of the World.* I thought of our new granddaughter and the Thanksgiving celebrations going on back home. Meanwhile, our three communist guards looked on with stony faces, and I became concerned over our boldness in talking about Jesus. Suddenly an older man, dressed in a soldier's overcoat, stepped very close to my face and asked, "Who is the tall, American-looking boy that always goes everywhere with you when you go out?"

There are no Americans anywhere in the area where we live. He could see Nick in our classroom, so he knew the "boy" he asked about wasn't my husband. I couldn't think of whom he might mean. And then the question went around the circle, with others asking the same thing. In various levels of English and in sometimes difficult-to-understand accents, many of them asked, "Yes, who is the tall American boy that goes with you? We have seen him with you as you walk from

class to class and when you are headed out the campus gates to go shopping."

I had no answer. Any boys who go with us in China look very Chinese—and most of them are short!

I came home from class still wondering, but as I awoke this morning the answer came to me. Many years ago when I was just a little girl I remember my dear Auntie Ruth teaching me the good news of Psalm 34:7.

I prayed, "Oh, Thank You God, for the best Thanksgiving ever!"

I'm not sure just what a guardian angel looks like, but I feel convinced that mine looks like a tall American boy and has been seen by many Chinese eyes. And I believe that God provided a tall American boy to hold the door open for the entrance of gospel light in China.

# CHAPTER
## 4

# A Canopy of Angel Wings

Have you ever thought of angels' wings serving as a tent or canopy to protect God's praying children? Here is Alma Wells's story. She lives today in Kelowna, British Columbia, but this experience happened when she was a farm girl on the plains of Alberta, Canada.

I am eighty years old, but I wish to relate an experience that took place when I was around thirteen or fourteen, which I recall as though it just happened yesterday.

My father was blind. He felt it was useless to rent pasture for our horses when they could be of use on the Hughes's farm near Didsbury, Alberta, about eight miles south of Olds.

It was a difficult task for me to harness them, though it was my job. Rudolph was a big horse for me to put the collar and harness on. I had to stand on a crate to do it. Daisy was less trouble.

Around noon I finally started out. We lived in the south end of Olds. I needed to go north one block to cross the railway tracks and then west one mile, then south.

I enjoyed the scenery as we passed a field of barley, ready to be harvested.

Then I heard a strange rumbling sound in the west. I had not noticed dark clouds or any indication of trouble. Then I saw it. Thick sheets of hail were rapidly advancing toward us eastward across the field. We could hear the hail bouncing and battering as it approached.

Rudolph and Daisy were flighty horses, so I expected trouble. As I saw the hail coming, I prayed that the Lord would protect the horses. I feared Dad's wrath over any damage we might suffer, so indirectly I was praying for myself, too.

Then the hail struck all around us, and I cringed, expecting to be hurt. But not a pellet struck us. I looked at the horses, which trotted along as if everything was normal. Then I looked at my feet, and in the back of the wagon, but there was not one hailstone, though we were now surrounded by the storm, rushing and rattling like a barrage of ice bullets.

Then I looked up. The hail came to a point, then parted as if we were in a tent, and I praised God for His divine protection. Though I held the reins in my hands I knew I had no control of the horses.

Then another thought struck me, and I again sent up a prayer. We were approaching the railway crossing, and the 12:30 passenger train coming in to Olds was due about then. I could not see anything because of the hail, and its noise prevented me from hearing the train whistle. We bumped over the tracks, and then I noticed the dark form of the engine approaching behind us. It roared past moments after our crossing.

With tears coursing down my cheeks, I praised our great Protector and had a story to tell when I arrived at the Hughes's home. We all praised God together.

The next day when I returned, that beautiful field of barley was pounded into the ground as though it had been turned by a disc. Lightning had splintered a power pole. I still don't understand why dark clouds or other warnings of a hailstorm had not appeared. When I get to heaven I want to learn what ingenious method the angel used to spare us from harm that day. Meanwhile, this experience has helped me through some difficult times.

CHAPTER
5

# Helped by an Angel

Truly our lives are interwoven with those of angels. This is especially true of those who love God and wish to serve Him faithfully, as an expression of gratitude for His salvation. "For the eyes of the Lord run to and fro throughout the whole earth, to show Himself strong on behalf of those whose heart is loyal to Him" (2 Chronicles 16:9). And often He mediates that strength through His angels, who are always ready to do His bidding.

Ardythe Hovland of Aiea, Hawaii tells this story about her father-in-law, Halvor Hovland. This story has greatly strengthened the Hovland family's faith down through the years. Ardythe herself heard it from Halvor.

In the early 1900s the Hovland family moved to a farm near Eldon, Missouri. Some time during this period, Halvor had an experience that he loved to recount with awe. It was harvest time, and in those days farmers cut their grain with a scythe. One cloudy Friday afternoon, when the grain was perfectly ripe, Mr. Fogelman, a neighbor, came over and said, "Halvor, you'll have to cut your crop tomorrow, or it will go down on you."

From a farmer's standpoint Mr. Fogelman's words made sense. For, when the grain becomes over-ripe, the weight of the heads makes it lie down flat in the field,

thus making it impossible to reap. An entire crop can be lost this way.

Halvor's reply was, "Well, it will just have to 'go down' then, Mr. Fogelman, because tomorrow is Saturday, the seventh-day Sabbath, and the Fourth Commandment tells us to do no work on that day. I'll trust in God and harvest my grain the next day."

"You're crazy!" Fogelman responded. "It's cloudy now, and by tomorrow it might even rain. You'd better get an early start tomorrow morning, Sabbath or no Sabbath." But Halvor remained firm in his convictions; he prayed that the storm clouds would pass over and that the ripened grain would remain standing until Sunday.

His prayer was answered, and all day Sunday he worked under the hot sun, cutting swath after swath of grain with his scythe. He hardly stopped to rest, and by nightfall, instead of getting only one-half the crop harvested, he was surprised to find that he had been able to cover the entire field!

> *I've always known you as a man of your word, now tell me, who did you get to help you?*

When he went to the house, he told his wife, Carrie, that he was very thankful to have the crop all cut and was amazed that he had been able to do so much in just one day.

On Monday morning, Mr. Fogelman was back again. "Well, Halvor, I see you got all your grain cut. But where did you find someone to help you on a Sunday? You know we're all strict Sunday-keepers around here, and I didn't know of anyone available for hire on that day."

"What do you mean?" Halvor said. "No one helped me. I did it all by myself."

Fogelman said, "Now, Halvor, I've always known you as a man of your word, and you have never lied to me in all the years you've lived here, so don't start now. You know good and well that it takes two days to cut that field of grain, and here it is all done in one day. Now tell me, who did you get to help you?"

Halvor again replied, "No one, I'm telling you. No one helped me."

By this time, Mr. Fogelman was puzzled and said, "Halvor, I know what I saw. There was a man who followed you all day long. He walked right behind you. I watched him from my kitchen window. He had a scythe just like yours, and when you cut a swath, he would cut a swath. When you stopped to clean your scythe, he would stop and clean his scythe. When you stopped to rest, he would stop."

Halvor loved to tell this story to his children and grandchildren and would always finish by reading this verse in the Bible: "The angel of the Lord encamps around those who fear Him" (Psalm 34:7, NASB).

He also often quoted Isaiah 58:13, 14: "If because of the sabbath, you turn your foot From doing your own pleasure on My holy day, And call the sabbath a delight, the holy day of the Lord honorable, And shall honor it, desisting from your own ways, From seeking your own pleasure, And speaking your own word, Then you will take delight in the Lord, And I will make you ride on the heights of the earth; And I will feed you with the heritage of Jacob your father, For the mouth of the Lord has spoken" (NASB).

# CHAPTER
# 6

# Triumph Out of Tragedy

Carol Holley of Delta Junction, Alaska, tells the story of how angels brought triumph out of tragedy in her life. Carol writes:

On July 25, 1992, my husband and I had traveled 100 miles to Fairbanks, Alaska, to pick up my parents, who were coming for a visit. Even though we were driving home a little after midnight, it was still light. The sun had just dipped below the horizon.

About fifteen miles from home we were driving through a swampy area with a slight drop-off on the right side of the road when suddenly a moose sprang onto the road. I don't think my husband even got his foot off the accelerator. It felt as though we hit a brick wall. Then I was aware of a tremendous weight in my lap. I slowly opened my eyes—it was the windshield.

Except for a cut on my arm, I was OK. My husband was killed instantly. We were driving a small Saab with a sunroof that was slightly open at the time. The front of the car apparently knocked the moose off its feet, and it landed on the strip of the roof between the top of the windshield and the sunroof. That strip of metal crashed into the front seat, hitting my husband's head.

A couple of weeks later, the smashed car was towed to my house and left out by the garage. In my attempt to make some sense out of the greatest tragedy of my life, I went out to examine the car. I swept away enough glass to sit once again in the passenger's seat and saw something that made me think that there may really be a God. The strip of metal that had come crashing in, killing my husband, had conformed around my head without the slightest contact. From where I was sitting in that car, there was only about an inch of space where the metal had wrapped itself around my head.

Even then, in my pagan mindset, the only explanation I could think of was that an angel had reached down and put his hand in front of my face, and the metal just went around.

Now, all these years later, I have no doubt this is what happened. God had to take drastic measures to reach me, and it worked.

I am now a leader in my local church, and my son was baptized two years ago in the Jordan River. Considering my negative attitude toward Christianity when my son was young, this is truly a miracle.

I pray that someday I can thank that angel face to face. As I think back on my life, it took the death of two men to save me—Jesus for my salvation, and my husband, to bring me to a point of openness to Christ for salvation and relief from pain.

"In all their affliction He was afflicted, And the angel of His presence saved them; In His love and in His mercy He redeemed them; And He lifted them and carried them all the days of old" (Isaiah 63:9, NASB).

# An Angel Ministers to Jesus

No account of angelic support matches the poignancy of Christ's experience in Gethsemane. In that secluded garden at the foot of Mount Olivet, Jesus agonized over the price He must pay to ransom and redeem the human race. All heaven watched in suspense to see what decision He would make in the face of Satan's supernaturally skillful tactics. Is it any wonder that He prayed, "My Father, if it is possible, may this cup be taken from me" (Matthew 26:39)?

In the extremity of His anguish and spiritual separation from the Father, the Just suffering for the unjust, Jesus sweat great drops of blood and came close to dying from the crushing weight of supernatural grief. Then something marvelous happened in that Garden where our Lord groaned and pleaded with God for some alternative way—even though He knew in His heart it could not be. The Father sent an angel to help Christ drink the cup of suffering and judgment on our behalf, that He might be able to offer with nail-pierced hands the cup of salvation and joy to us.

With clarity of insight, the author of *The Desire of Ages* described this crucial juncture of Christ's ordeal in these words:

"Angels had longed to bring relief to the divine sufferer, but this might not be. No way of escape was found for the Son of God. In this awful crisis, when every-

thing was at stake, when the mysterious cup trembled in the hand of the sufferer, the heavens opened, a light shone forth amid the stormy darkness of the crisis hour, and the mighty angel who stands in God's presence, occupying the position from which Satan fell, came to the side of Christ. The angel came not to take the cup from Christ's hand, but to strengthen Him to drink it, with the assurance of the Father's love. He came to give power to the divine-human suppliant. He pointed Him to the open heavens, telling Him of the souls that would be saved as the result of His sufferings. He assured Him that His Father is greater and more powerful than Satan, that His death would result in the utter discomfiture of Satan, and that the kingdom of this world would be given to the saints of the Most High. He told Him that He would see the travail of His soul and be satisfied, for He would see a multitude of the human race saved, eternally saved" (Ellen White, *The Desire of Ages*, pp. 693, 694).

# Their Highest Pleasure

*"Are they not all ministering spirits, sent forth to minister for them*
*who shall be heirs of salvation?"*
Hebrews 1:14, KJV.

For our Father in His wisdom knows the weakness of our frame—

Knows our adversary's strength and subtle power;

And in tender love and mercy sends the angels in His name

To sustain and keep us in temptation's hour.

Angels find their highest pleasure in this work for fallen man,

Dwelling with us 'mid earth's saddest scenes below;

Working in cooperation with their loved Commander's plan

To uplift and save the world from sin and woe.

—A. M. Williams

# Angel Assurance

Christ wishes to give those who trust Him full assurance of faith, the very blessing that Satan most dreads our having. Josephine B. of Williamsport, Maryland tells the story of how angels worked in a special way to bring comfort to her mother at a crucial period in her life.

My ninety-eight-year-old mother, Hilah, was almost blind and had life-threatening health problems, when she discovered that she was afraid of dying. This seemed strange to us, considering her faithful, lifelong commitment to God. Yet I have discovered that many Christians are shaky about their assurance of salvation.

I talked and prayed with my mother, and read Bible verses to her about trust in God—verses such as Psalm 56:3, 4. "When I am afraid, I will trust in you. In God, whose word I praise, in God I trust; I will not be afraid" (NIV). One evening Mother had a spell during which it seemed that her heart almost stopped. We were greatly relieved to see this episode pass, as her heartbeat returned to normal. I didn't know what her feelings were, but the next morning when she awoke, she asked excitedly, "Did you see all the angels?"

I looked at her a little puzzled, and she continued, "Oh, my, all those angels I saw!" Then as she realized that my dad and I had not seen what she had seen, she said to us, "I wish you all could see them! They all looked as though they were coming down to welcome me."

She related with joy that during the previous night she had been in the back yard (which was surely a fantasy or a dream, for she had not been outside the house), and all of a sudden the sky was full of angels! She described how the angels were circling around, filling the sky with their beauty and brightness. Then they came very near to her, and she felt their power. She supposed that they had come to take her away, but they did not. After a while they went back into heaven.

"It's going to be grand!" she exclaimed, thinking of the time when the angels actually will come with Jesus to take the redeemed to be with Him. She sang a snatch of the song, We'll Never Say Good-bye in Heaven which I hadn't heard for years. A little later she sang, in her very elderly voice, Jesus Is the Sweetest Name I Know.

Hilah loved to relate this experience of seeing the angels. I think that God gave her a vision of angels to let her know how much He loved her and that she had nothing to fear. She continued to be highly motivated to live, and passed her one hundredth birthday, but she never again gave indication that she feared death!

# The Traveling Companion

Jesus has promised never to leave us nor forsake us. This promise is sure, and we certainly do need its support in times of difficulty and danger.

John F., a pastor, was traveling alone from Wyoming to his new pastorate in New Jersey. This journey was the most sorrowful of all his life. His beloved wife had gone spiritually adrift and ended their marriage in order to take up with a same-sex companion. Fifteen years of marriage and service together had turned to dust. Never had life seemed so desolate and lonely. Pastor John had to move to a completely new area—away from the pain and loss, away from the consternation of grieving church members who felt as helpless in the face of this tragedy as he did.

Knowing the journey was long, Pastor John wanted to cover as many miles as he could each day. He prayed that God would be by his side all the way and send an angel to keep his misting eyes from blinding him with tears. He prayed for comfort, and it came. From time to time as he crossed the vast expanse of his beloved Wyoming he felt the sustaining presence of a divine being with him. He was able to look forward to the future with some hope.

As John came toward the eastern end of Wyoming he felt very tired. He saw a sign indicating that a motel and diner lay seventeen miles ahead in Bushnell,

Nebraska. That's where I'll stop, John decided. I'll spend the night. If only I can hold out until then; I'm so tired, he thought. Oh, Lord, be with me, he prayed. Moments later John fell asleep at the wheel.

The next thing he knew, a voice called to him, "Wake up, John." Startled, he looked ahead and saw himself cruising along the road at the allowed speed. His hands were firmly on the wheel. Immediately to the right a sign appeared that read, "Bushnell Exit 1/2 mile." By now John was really awake. It struck him: I've been sleeping for the past fifteen miles or so. Thank You Lord for preserving my life.

Pulling off at the exit, John went to the nearest gas station. Two attendants were sitting outside, smoking and chatting on this summer's night. Ambling over to the car a few moments later, one filled the tank while the other washed the car windows. Learning from the attendant where the nearest motel was, John paid him and said good night.

> *"Oh, Lord, be with me," he prayed. Moments later John fell asleep at the wheel.*

"Just a minute, sir," the attendant said, concern written on his face. "Where's the other fellow that was with you? Did he go to the restroom? You don't want to leave him behind, do you?"

"What fellow?" John asked.

"You know, that young blond guy that was sitting next to you in the passenger's seat. My partner and I both saw him as you drove in."

John knew that the attendant had seen his angel, while he himself was only dimly and sporadically aware of his presence. But how could he explain this to the puzzled attendant? "Oh, he's my traveling companion. Sometimes you can see him, and sometimes he's invisible."

"Oh, I see. Sure, mister, sure. You have a good night now," said the attendant, uneasily backing away. But John just smiled. He knew who was in the seat beside him.

CHAPTER
# 10

# The Mystery of the Silver Dollar

One of the primary tasks of angels seems to be to cooperate with God for the salvation of human beings. One of the most creative strategies used by an angel to help in this process appears in this story related by Arthur S. Maxwell.

Many years ago, about 1896 or 1897, a Christian man who sold books and Bibles door to door was walking down Market Street in San Francisco when a stranger stopped him and asked him why he did not take his Bibles and books to a certain valley beyond Sacramento. The bookseller explained that he had never heard of the valley but would be glad to go when he could find the time. Then the stranger bade him goodbye, and disappeared in the crowd.

That's strange! the man thought to himself. I wonder why that man spoke to me. How did he know my business? And why is he interested in that particular valley? I must try to go there someday. But the busy days and weeks slipped by, and the bookseller didn't go. Yet somehow he couldn't forget what the stranger had said. Every now and then a voice seemed to say to him, "Go to that valley."

At last he felt he should wait no longer. So he set forth on his journey, taking his Bibles and other books with him. It was a long and tiring trip, for there were no autos in those days. Part of the way he went by train, part on horseback, part on foot. Coming to a wide river, which had not then been bridged, he wondered how he was going to get to the other side. As he waited at the water's edge a man appeared in a rowboat and asked if he wished to cross.

"I surely do," said the bookseller. "How much will you charge to take me over?"

"A dollar," replied the man in the boat, and the other man agreed.

On the way across, the bookseller opened his purse and brought out a silver dollar. It was the only one he had and, having time on his hands, he looked at it with more than usual care. It was a new coin, bright from the mint, but marred by a scratch on the eagle. The date on the coin was 1896. Arriving at the other side, he gave the boatman the silver dollar and bade him goodbye.

"Be sure to call at the first cottage you come to up the valley," called the boatman as he turned the boat back into the river.

"I will," replied the bookseller, wondering what this might mean and what he would find there.

Soon he caught sight of a cottage on a hillside about a mile ahead and walked briskly toward it. To his surprise, as he drew near the cottage, the front door opened and three children started running down the hill toward him.

> *I opened the door and there, lying on the ground, was a silver dollar.*

"Did you bring our Bible?" they cried. "Did you bring our Bible?"

"Your Bible!" he exclaimed. "What do you mean? How did you know I have some Bibles?"

"Oh," they cried, "we've all been praying for a Bible, but Mother didn't have the money to buy one till today. But God sent her the money, so we felt sure He would send us the Bible soon."

By this time they were at the house, and the mother came out, all flushed and excited, waiting to tell her story of what had happened. "It's true," she said. "We

have wanted a Bible so long. We've been praying for one for many months but somehow could never afford it. Then this afternoon, just after we had all prayed again, a voice seemed to say to me, 'Go and look out the front door.' So I opened the door and there, lying on the ground, was a silver dollar. It seemed so wonderful that I felt sure God had sent it, and that the Bible would come soon. Sir, does your Bible cost a dollar?"

"It does," he replied. "Just a dollar."

Opening his case, he took out a Bible and handed it to the mother, who in turn passed over to him the dollar she had found beside her door that very afternoon.

Now it was the bookseller's turn to be astonished. Something about the dollar arrested his attention. It was newly minted, but had a scratch on the eagle. And the date was 1896!

"Is there something wrong with it?" asked the mother anxiously.

"No, no," he said. "But, madam, this is the identical dollar I gave to the boatman this very afternoon, less than an hour ago!"

"What boatman?" she asked.

"At the ferry."

"But there's no ferry; never has been, as long as I've been here."

"But he brought me across the river this very afternoon and told me to come to this cottage; and I gave him this same silver dollar!"

So they talked on, going over it all again and again, marveling at how God works, "His wonders to perform."

The mystery of that silver dollar will perhaps never be solved. But both the bookseller and that godly woman were convinced, as I am, that God was in this thing. He knew of the longing of the dear mother and her children to read His Word; and in His own wonderful way He made it possible for them to receive it.

And if you wonder about the stranger and boatman, remember that Abraham of old "entertained angels unawares."—Adapted from Arthur S. Maxwell, *Bedtime Stories*, (Pacific Press, 1976) vol. 4, pp. 157-160.

CHAPTER

# 11

# A Young Man With Special Ears

Wherever Jesus walked, throngs of suffering people came to Him for deliverance from their infirmities of mind and body. Jesus delighted in placing His healing touch on them. He went about in Galilee "healing every kind of disease and every kind of sickness among the people. And the news about Him went out into all Syria; and they brought to Him all that were ill, taken with various diseases and pains, demoniacs, epileptics, paralytics; and He healed them" (Matthew 4:23, 24, NASB).

Angels serve as living extensions of God's will. Their hands and faculties are at His command. It is no wonder then that we should find them frequently acting as agents to heal and restore those who reach out to God and for whom special prayer is offered.

Cyril Miller, a Christian pastor, writes of his experience with angels and their healing power.

Traveling late one night on a narrow rural highway, I met with a near-fatal accident. A semi truck swung into my lane with blinding lights and then swerved sharply to the left to make a quick turn into a driveway, thus leaving the trailer squarely in my lane.

Automatically applying the brakes, I jerked my car to the right toward the ditch, but it was too late. Crashing headlong into the trailer, I found myself pinned by the car's motor, which had been thrust into the front seat.

I awakened to hear the excitement of people trying to free me from the wreckage. One man was shouting, "We will have to cut off his foot to get him out." I pleaded, "Please do not cut off my foot," and prayed, "Dear Lord, don't let them cut off my foot."

The motor was jacked up, thereby freeing me, and the top of my automobile was torn away with a "jaws of life" rescue machine. Then I was removed, placed inside a helicopter, and flown to a major hospital in the city nearby.

Still conscious upon arrival, I asked the attending nurse for pen and paper. I gave her a message for the doctor, which simply said, "Please do not amputate my foot." Immediately I became unconscious and stayed that way for nearly a month. While in a coma, it seemed as if I was in a dark cave. I could hear people talking but could see nothing. I even heard the doctors and nurses say, "He isn't going to make it."

In addition to a crushed right foot and lower leg, I had multiple fractures in my arm, which were never set; crushed ribs; flayed lungs; and other injuries. Additional complications resulted when I developed bacterial pneumonia and a staphylococcic infection in my wounds during the time I was unconscious.

Four weeks later I awakened to discover that God had miraculously spared my life as an answer to many prayers by friends everywhere. One night, when it appeared that I might not live through the night, three ministers came and anointed me as the Bible instructs in James 5:14.

From then on I made steady progress, except that I still had many life support tubes all over my body. Tubes were in my arms for medication, my stomach for nourishment, my bladder for voiding, my lungs for draining, and my throat for breathing.

Actually, I was on respirator support during the four weeks of unconsciousness and the fifth week after awakening. One evening the pulmonary specialist came by and said, "Your lungs may not come back."

I asked, "What does that mean?"

He replied, "You will be short of breath the rest of your life."

Though unable at this time to breathe without the respirator, I didn't recognize how bad the prognosis was. Engulfed in deep depression, I thought, *I'll never be the same again, not being able to preach or even talk without difficulty.*

A few evenings later, a young man whom I had never seen before, came to my room. In a very assuring, authoritative voice, he said, "I have special ears; I can hear things that no one else can hear."

As he began to place the stethoscope on my chest, I asked, "What do you hear?"

He answered, "I hear a free flow of air through every lobe of your lungs."

I looked out in the hall and saw Joyce, who is now my wife, waiting. I motioned for her to come into the room. After introducing her to the young man, I told her what he had just told me by saying, "He has special ears and can hear things that no one else can hear." He repeated the same words again: "I hear a free flow of air through every lobe of his lungs," and then he left quickly.

Later, my sister, her pastor husband, and my daughter came to visit me. I told them about the young man and what he had said. Since they had stayed very close—almost day and night during those critical weeks—and knew virtually everyone who came in and out of the room, they asked, "Who was he? What did he look like?"

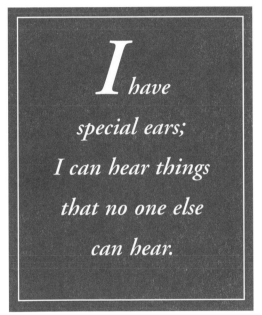

*I have special ears; I can hear things that no one else can hear.*

I replied, "He has never been here before. I can't describe him—except that he was a nice looking young man."

About a week later, I was reading in the book of Mark about the women who went to Jesus' tomb on the Resurrection morning and found it empty. It says that they looked inside the tomb and there sat "a young man" (Mark 16:5).

I said, "Wait a minute, what translation is this? I thought the Bible said an angel was at Jesus' tomb." Quickly turning to the front, I discovered it was the *King James Version.* So I turned to the other Gospels, where I discovered that the person in the tomb is called an angel.

I began to reflect upon all of this. Health professionals simply do not talk like that young man who said, "I have special ears, and I can hear things that no one else can hear." Also, my pulmonary specialist visited me about a week later and said, "Well, it looks as though your lungs are going to be OK," and I thought, *I already know that.*

Then I reasoned: "If angels appeared as young men in Bible times, then I may have seen my guardian angel." I had never seen this young man before, and I have never seen him since this unusual experience.

I was telling a friend of mine about my remarkable encounter and the conviction that it must have been an angel, and he replied, "Well Cyril, you may have seen your guardian angel. If he doesn't send you a bill, it probably was."

One of my attending physicians, an infection specialist, the one who had said, "He isn't going to make it," later acknowledged that I was healed by "divine intervention."

I thank God for saving my life and restoring my health. I also thank Him for dispatching one of His "ministering spirits" (Hebrews 1:14) to assure me and give me peace of mind that I would be all right, at a time when I most needed support.

It has been about four years since my accident, and I am able to routinely perform my administrative and ministerial work, which I greatly enjoy—especially preaching God's Word.

# 12

# Healed to Serve Others

Here is a story from J. H. Zachary, international evangelism coordinator for The Quiet Hour radio broadcast. It illustrates an angel's part in healing a man who then used his restored health to become a partner with angels in leading others to the Great Physician, Jesus, for the healing of the soul from its ultimate affliction—sin.

Vasele Lupu looked up from his hospital bed into the eyes of his son, Benone. "It's not good news," he said quietly. "The doctor says the cancer might have spread. But I have placed my life in God's hands. I am ready to live or die as He wills."

The two men prayed together in the hospital room in Bucharest, Romania. Then Benone left. Two days later when he returned to visit his father, he found him preparing to go home.

"What happened?" the younger man asked. "You were so ill!"

"I may have been dreaming," the older man told his son. "But after you left I saw an intense light at the foot of my bed. A man standing in the light told me that God had a work for me to do. Later I asked my roommate if he had seen a bright light or heard a voice during the night, but he had seen and heard nothing.

Surely I have been visited by an angel!"

Lupu, now healed and full of vitality, asked God to show him the ministry He had for him. He began visiting the prison in Bucharest, where he had spent several years as a prisoner for his faith during Communist times. He recognized many of the guards, and he remembered the insults that he had endured from guards and prisoners alike because of his faith. One guard recognized him and hurled new insults at him.

Lupu began sharing with the prisoners the message of hope in Christ. The guard who had insulted him listened to Lupu's testimony. His heart was touched, and he accepted Christ as his Savior.

But the guard's wife was angry about his decision. "How can an intelligent person believe there is a God?" she demanded. Then she challenged her husband. "Do you see this plant? It has never blossomed. If your God can make this plant bloom, then I will believe!"

Later that day the woman walked into the room where the barren plant sat. She stared at it amazed, for the plant was blooming! Faith blossomed in her heart, and she joined her husband to worship God and later followed him in baptism.

Lupu thanks God for giving him a special work to do.

Today, whether, you are sick or well, healed or bearing the cross of an infirmity, remember that angels wish to join you as partners in making known the Savior. Through His gospel all disease will ultimately be banished, and He will take His redeemed to a kingdom where the inhabitants will never say, "I am sick," but will revel in the abundance of health that pervades their bodies and souls. In the meantime, Christ will bear your infirmities, either by removing them, or as is sometimes more precious, by giving you grace to endure them, so that whether by life or by death, His love may be magnified in you.

# CHAPTER

# 13

# I Felt an Angel's Hands

Marie-Eve Renaud was glad to be heading away from downtown Montreal one sunny July afternoon. Ordinarily she avoided such trips for fear of the traffic. But she had to buy a computer at a downtown store.

Marie-Eve wanted to take the Metro, but her sister Annie persuaded her to drive, with the offer to go along. On their way home they drove through a tunnel from which their turn lane emerged.

Marie-Eve tells the rest of the story in her own words:

"You're in the wrong lane," Annie said. "We have to go east." I quickly pulled the car into the left lane, just as a few other cars pulled in behind me. I was the first to reach the stoplight. Seconds later there was a loud, terrible noise—a crashing, crunching sound I'd never heard before. Annie and I clapped our hands over our ears. "What was that?" I shouted. Annie looked bewildered.

I peered through the windshield and then glanced in my rearview mirror. All the drivers behind me had turned to look back. What's happened? Somehow I felt I had to see.

The light was still red in front of us. "Park the car!" I said to my sister, opening the door and stepping out. I turned to run up the street. I couldn't believe

what I saw. A huge cement truck was hanging halfway off the viaduct overhead, its front wheels spinning in the air! Part of the bridge had shattered under the weight of the truck, sending a giant slab of concrete plunging through the roof of a car standing alone in the street below. The passenger side of the car had been crushed.

I stood wondering what to do as cars sped past me. I stared up at the truck. A strange orange liquid poured from it onto the wrecked car.

The people around me seemed frozen in place. Go to the car, I told myself. As I crossed the street I could see a middle-aged man in the driver's seat. He was pounding frantically at the window, pushing on the door, trying to get out. I grabbed the handle and pulled. It wouldn't budge. I pulled again. Nothing.

I glanced around ... street. "Help me!" I ... The orange liquid ... sticking in my hair. ... crashed down. ... done. Fast! That ... minute. I turned back ... get a grip on the top ... window. I jammed ... into the narrow space ... frame meets the roof.

"Somebody help ...

*More concrete from the overpass fell, crushing the driver's side of the car.*

... at the people on the ... cried. No one moved. ... was falling on the car, ... More concrete ... Something had to be ... truck could fall any ... to the car and tried to ... of the driver's door ... the tips of my fingers ... where the window ... This is impossible! ... me!" I called again.

Instantly there were hands next to mine. But the strong hands pressed against the door while I was trying to pull it open. My fingers were being squeezed. "Whoa!" I said. "You're hurting me!"

The hands pushed harder. So I pushed in too and then quickly pulled back, hoping to pop the door open. Maybe there was air pressure inside the car. If the pressure were released somehow, maybe the door would open.

No one was near me, but I could feel the hands next to mine. Together we worked to free the trapped man. Crash! A window broke! Not the driver's window—the one in back! Glass shattered, but the shards didn't hit the man or me.

# ANGELS AMONG US

I grabbed the driver's door handle. It opened! I tried pulling the man to his feet.

He stood up, but I fell backward, and my arms came away from him just as a piece of concrete landed between us. People continued to keep their distance. Maybe the hands that helped me kept them away so no one would be hurt.

I grabbed the man's arm, and we hurried to the other side of the street. A sound like thunder shuddered behind us, and we turned. More concrete from the overpass had fallen, crushing the driver's side of the car. I caught my breath. We had escaped just in time.

I leaned the man against the supporting wall of the bridge. Nothing will collapse here next to the pillars. "Are you all right?" I asked. He nodded. "I thought I'd drown in what was leaking from the truck," he said, "or be crushed before you got me out."

"It wasn't just me," I said. "I had help."

"No one else came to the car," the man replied, shaking his head. "Only you."

There wasn't time to explain what I meant. Flashing lights and sirens announced the arrival of the police. After making sure the man was in their care, I left to find my sister.

Annie had parked on Rue St. Antoine. She looked shocked when she saw me approaching. I was covered with orange liquid from the truck, and my hair was matted against my face. Annie had some extra clothes in the car, so I changed before we started back. "This time, you drive," I insisted.

At home, I tried describing everything to my family. "There's no way I could have freed that man alone," I said. Even physics couldn't explain it. Someone was right there with me. I've always known my guardian angel was nearby. That day I felt his hands.—Adapted from Marie-Eve Renaud, *Angels on Earth*, March/April 1999.

# Two Angels in a Boat

Desmond Doss, a medic during World War II, fearlessly performed many rescue operations in the Pacific theater. His most amazing exploit involved the rescue of seventy-five soldiers, lowering them over a steep cliff to safety while enemy bullets flew around him, sometimes coming so close he could feel them streaking by.

President Truman decorated Desmond Doss with the Congressional Medal of Honor on the White House lawn for his unwavering valor in the face of extreme danger. But Doss would not have been around to rescue those seventy-five soldiers had he not been rescued himself several years before the war.

Desmond and his young nephew Gary were playing on a beach along the Atlantic coast. Gary's new beach ball somehow got away from him and began drifting out to sea. Though not a very good swimmer, Desmond could not refuse his little nephew's appeal for him to go out and retrieve the ball. Desmond swam through the shallow water for a few hundred feet before he realized that the widening distance between himself and the ball was due to a strongly ebbing tide.

A feeling of desperation washed over him. He knew it would be impossible to swim against the tide back to shore. If only he could catch up with the ball, then he could hold on to it as a kind of life preserver, but it was getting farther from him each moment. But Desmond was used to praying, so he offered up this simple plea: "Lord, help me!"

Desmond looked about. He could hardly be seen now from the receding shore, and the ball was now drifting from his sight. But then something else came into view—a small motorized fishing boat. The two men in the boat appeared to be pulling in fishing nets and preparing to go farther out in the ocean. Desmond prayed that they would notice him. He called out but realized that the boat's engine drowned out his voice.

Then the fishermen spotted the big beach ball coming their way. One of them bent over the side of the boat and retrieved the ball. Peering around, they also spotted Desmond and immediately came to his rescue. One of the men reached over the side of the boat and said, "Let me help you in."

Soon the boat drew close to shore. The other fisherman asked, "Can you make it from here?" The water was shallow, so, thanking the men, Desmond stepped out and waded ashore with his nephew's beach ball. On the beach he turned to wave at his rescuers, but there were no men, no boat, not even the wake of the boat's path through the sea. To this day, Desmond Doss believes that angels rescued him from drowning.

# Angel Hands

Karen L. of Anderson, California relates this story.

It was a beautiful afternoon in March 1984. We were living in Napa, California. My six children, my husband and I were on a ride in our Chevy station wagon. We had driven over to the ocean and were headed back home, singing as we went. It had been a perfect day and the sun would soon be setting.

As we cruised along a country road at about forty mph, we saw a huge buck standing beside the road. It started to bound into the woods, but suddenly turned back and came straight across the road. My husband slammed on the brakes, but we knew it was too late. The deer tried to jump over the hood but it didn't jump high enough. We knew that if we hit the buck, it would come through the windshield.

Suddenly the deer was picked up and lifted over the car. It was high enough that on its undersides we could see the perfect imprints of two hands. It was as if everything went into slow motion. All of us in the car were able to see it. My husband, Bruce, stopped the car, and we all sat still for a bit, marveling at what we had just seen.

That day will always be special to us, the day we saw the angel hands.

God's promise is dependable: "He shall give his angels charge over thee, to keep thee in all thy ways. They shall bear thee up in their hands" (Psalm 91:11, 12, KJV). Or, if necessary, they will bear up a deer to keep it from causing an accident.

# CHAPTER 16

# A Mother's Prayer

Angels are not only good bodyguards; they are also talented at guiding our footsteps into the paths of righteousness. They read character and warn us against being lured into evil company that would pollute our minds or bodies. God's promise is, "Behold, I send an Angel before you to keep you in the way and to bring you into the place which I have prepared" (Exodus 23:20). Ultimately, that place is heaven, and all along the way, God wishes us to spiritually live in heavenly places through Christ Jesus (see Ephesians 2:6).

God knew a little girl who loved Jesus and needed His special protection in order to maintain her heaven-bound purity. Marie Johnson of Coquille, Oregon tells us about this little girl, a relative of hers from an earlier generation.

Jessie was three years old when her mother took her to the lumber camp where Grandma and the aunties lived. Mama was expecting a new baby, and in the early days of the twentieth century it was customary to be with family at such a time.

The camp was a rowdy place—rough men doing rough work, and wild teen-aged boy cousins running in a pack. It was daunting for a three-year old.

One quiet summer afternoon Jessie was kneeling in the path in the middle of the camp, running her little cars on the roads she had carved in the dust. Glancing up, she saw her angel walk around the corner of the house and approach her. Jessie's mother had told her about angels, about her angel who always watched over her. Instinctively she recognized him as her own. He stopped beside her and held out his hand. Jessie rose to her feet, took his hand and walked with him down the path into the woods. The path led to the wreck of an old cabin. They approached it and the angel lifted Jessie up so she could see through the window.

She could see herself inside the cabin, surrounded by her rough cousins. They were molesting her. "Don't come here with those boys," the angel instructed her. "They will hurt you." He lowered her to the ground, and the next thing Jessie knew, she was again running her little cars on their dusty roads.

A few minutes later her cousins came roistering down the path. "Hey, Jessie, come with us," they called.

"No."

"Aw, c'mon, Jess. We got somethin' to show you."

"No."

"We got candy in the old cabin. Want some?"

"No!" Jessie answered with such force that the boys glanced nervously about to see if an adult had heard. They slunk silently away, and those boys didn't bother Jessie again that summer.

This experience became more precious to Jessie as she matured and realized how special it was. She cherished it in her heart, but she was a grown woman with children of her own before she mentioned it to a soul. One day she confided the experience to her mother.

"Oh, darling," her mother replied. "I was so worried about you that summer. I knew those were vile boys, and I begged God to protect you. How wonderfully

> "*Don't come here with those boys,*" *the angel instructed her.*

He answered my prayers! And I'm glad that I had told you about your special angel so you recognized him when he came to you."

Angels linger where purity is sought, and where the love of Jesus is welcomed as the ruling power of the life.

# CHAPTER
# 17

# Hearing the Angels Sing

The day was drawing to a close as Luella Crane and her two children, Mira, nine, and Bob, twelve, walked out of the back door of their home for sunset worship outdoors.

Their chairs stood at the back of the yard where the children had been playing during the week. Not too far away, behind this little nook, towering fir trees lifted their branches high above the mossy, fern-covered ground. That would be the perfect place for their devotions, Luella felt.

Generally, Luella's courage was good, but she had experienced overwhelming trials, trying to raise her small children alone since the tragic death of her husband some years before. This had been an especially trying week, and she found herself feeling discouraged.

As the three stepped outside, an unusual sky caught their attention with its rich golden hues filtering through the trees. Luella felt she had never seen such a brilliant yellow sky. The children noticed too, pausing with their mother to admire its breathtaking beauty.

Then the sound of music drifted down to them from the upper branches of those majestic trees. Softly it began with the sound of harps. Gradually it swelled into a rich symphonic orchestra. Then came the voices of singing—and such singing! Luella stood transfixed; it was the loveliest music she had ever heard!

Mira was frightened. Plainly, it was not a human orchestra and choir sounding from the treetops. And no one was visible as they looked up. Mira started to cry as she stood between her mother and her brother, Bob.

Luella slipped a comforting arm about her daughter, and Bob also reached an arm about his little sister. Then Luella spoke. "We must surely be hearing angels sing." It just had to be. As they listened in awestruck wonder, these words drifted down to them:

"Oh, Shepherd divine, I know Thou art mine: Thy search through the night was for me. This bleak world is cold, but warm is Thy fold. My Shepherd, I follow Thee."

The last golden notes faded into silence except for the voice of a night bird as the evening shadows fell. Returning to the house, Luella went at once to her piano. Her fingers flew across the keys as she attempted to recapture the melody they had just heard. Mira told me that her mother played it again and again.

We must surely be hearing angels sing.

Only a few years later, Herbert Work, a composer and music teacher wrote both the words and music to this same song the angels had sung that evening to Luella and her children. Among the many songs he had written, it seemed to Herbert Work that this one was his best.

At the time Herbert Work wrote this song he had not so much as heard of Luella or her experience. He told me his inspiration for songs always seemed to come to him when he was in the woods. He was behind a barn in northern

California, among the trees, when the inspiration came to him to write My Shepherd. It was just a quiet inspiration, nothing as dramatic as Luella and her children had encountered. But the music and the words were identical to those Luella and her children had heard several years earlier.—Adapted from "The Song," by Ida Mae Morley, *The North Pacific Union Gleaner*, May 5, 1990.

*"The angel of the Lord encampeth round about them
that fear him, and delivereth them."*
Psalm 34:7, *KJV*

# Faithful Angel Watchers

*There are faithful angel watchers with their wings above us spread,*

*Shielding us from unseen dangers night and day;*

*Prompting us to seek for guidance when unconsciously we tread*

*In the paths of hidden danger by the way.*

*Could the veil of mist be lifted and our mortal eyes behold*

*Silent records being taken of each scene,*

*How we'd guard our words and actions, many tales we'd leave untold,*

*And we'd strive to keep our records pure and clean.*

A. M. Williams

# An Angel Serenade

This story is not only a beautiful example of music in the ministry of angels, but it also provides an unusual glimpse into the conflict between good and evil angels, a conflict that rages over every person who commits his or her life to Christ. The story comes from Charlotte Ishkanian in *The Devil Tried.*

In 1994 three Christians went to live and work among the people on Hilantagaan, a tiny island that lies off the northern tip of the island of Cebu in central Philippines. Most of the islanders follow a religion that reveres a Filipino hero whom, they believe, was the reincarnation of Christ. Many of their beliefs mix elements of Christianity with occult practices. The Christians made friends, held Vacation Bible Schools, and shared their faith. Gradually, the people of the island began to open their hearts to these three lay workers. Some listened to their words of faith, and within a year, eight people were baptized.

The lay workers and the new believers laid plans to hold evangelistic meetings on the island. They asked the *barangay* [village] captain for permission to hold the meetings in the open-air plaza at the center of the largest village on the island. The *barangay* captain had a Christian relative, so he willingly gave permission.

But when the devil saw the progress Christians were making in his territory, he was angry. He tried all sorts of tricks to disrupt the meetings. On the day that the meetings were to begin, the speaker suddenly became ill and was taken to the hospital. That evening a church member stepped in and spoke. Suddenly the sound system went dead. The speaker continued with his presentation while the soundman searched for the problem in the equipment. He found a wire that had been yanked loose in the amplifier and quickly repaired it. But within a few minutes the system went dead again. The soundman found that *the same wire* had been pulled loose. Again he repaired the wire, but this time he stood nearby to be sure no one tampered with the amplifier. But within a few minutes the same wire was torn out again.

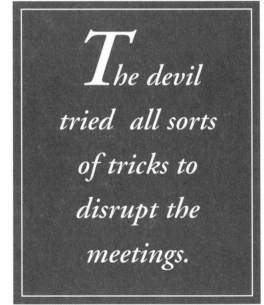

*The devil tried all sorts of tricks to disrupt the meetings.*

Realizing that no human hand had torn the wire out, a group of believers began praying that God would restrain Satan's hand and prevent him from disrupting the meetings. The rest of the evening the amplifier wires were not touched.

The next evening the devil again tore out the wire. But when the prayer band began praying, the devil's mischief ended. The believers realized that prayer was their only defense against demonic sabotage. But the members of the prayer group wanted to hear the speaker's message, so they stopped praying. Immediately, the devil returned to cause mischief. The prayer band realized that they had to continue praying or the devil would create havoc.

Many other strange things happened to plague the little band of workers. These supernatural manifestations did not seem to surprise the people of this island. They knew that evil spirits were causing these disturbances and even suggested that if the Christians appeased the spirits, they would stop their mischief!

Instead the believers prayed that God would show the people who was more powerful. The answer that came to encourage the band of harassed workers was most unusual.

The Filipino people enjoy the lovely custom of serenading. Very early in the morning, while it is still dark, friends gather under the window of the persons they wish to honor and will sing songs for them. The Christian believers on this island decided to form two serenading bands. They awoke about 3:00 A.M. each morning to serenade the islanders who were attending the meetings. The singing would awaken the people inside, who would then welcome the singers into the home for a brief visit, which always ended with prayer.

The believers tried to serenade several homes each day before dawn. But by the eighth night the group was simply too tired to wake up at 3:00 A.M. Suddenly the believers were awakened by the sound of beautiful singing. They hurried to the door and looked outside, but they could not see anyone. They dressed quickly and hurried toward the home of the other group of serenaders. On their way, they met the second group in the street. "Were you serenading us tonight?" they asked.

"No," the second group said. "You were serenading us!"

"No," the first group answered. "We overslept, and were awakened by beautiful singing! Was it not you?" All the believers had overslept, yet both groups had been serenaded. A hush fell over them as they realized that heavenly singers had serenaded them. With tears in their eyes, they hugged one another, grateful for the knowledge that God had blessed their efforts by sending His heavenly choir of angels to serenade and encourage them.

As the meetings ended, eighteen new believers were baptized. A second group soon joined them, and today some seventy members meet in a lovely little church that they built on their island. They have forsaken the superstitions that held them in bondage to Satan, and they continue to share their faith in the God who is stronger than the devil.

"He who dwells in the shelter of the Most High

will rest in the shadow of the Amighty.

I will say of the Lord, 'He is my refuge and my fortress,

my God, in whom I trust.' . . .

If you make the Most High your dwelling—

even the Lord, who is my refuge—

then no harm will befall you,

no disaster will come near your tent.

For he will command his angels concerning you

to guard you in all your ways;

they will lift you up in their hands,

so that you will not strike your foot against a stone."

—Psalm 91:1, 2, 9-12, NIV.

# An Angel on the Stairs

This story comes from a young girl, Elizabeth M., who was only nine years old when the story took place—and only fourteen when she related what happened.

In 1993, I was nine years old, and my sister, Ruth, was ten. One day my mother went to run some errands, and Ruth and I were home alone. After a while we got into an argument—I don't recall what our squabble was about. I stormed upstairs to the loft overlooking the family room. Our family room had a cathedral ceiling and a stairway leading into a loft that we used as a classroom for our home school.

Feeling bad about our fight, I sat at my study desk wanting to tell my sister that I was sorry and that I loved her. I thought about writing her a card. While pondering these thoughts, I also wondered if I was really sincere about my feelings. Heavy-hearted, I slowly began to make my way downstairs.

I saw an angel on the landing where the steps turn to the right. He was very tall, maybe nine or ten feet. I cannot adequately express the angel's appearance. It was too beautiful for ordinary words. He was bright and was surrounded by a shimmering light of transparent gold. In his left hand he held a sword pointed downwards. His countenance held an expression of displeasure. Not displeasure as we think of it. Not anger. I sensed his deep concern for my well-being and the decisions I would make. His goodness and love for me shone through, but still, feeling unfit to be in his presence, I couldn't help being scared.

With a wave of his sword, the angel motioned for me to go down. He seemed to know the choice I was about to make. Then he disappeared, and I ran quickly down the stairs, scraping my right arm against the railing. I dashed into my parents' room, and my sister entered a few moments later. Immediately noticing my injured arm, she asked me what had happened. I was too overwhelmed to tell her the story, but ran into the living room and hid behind a chair. My sister suggested that we go for a walk. During our walk I was able to tell her in little spurts what had happened. We both cried and told each other how sorry we were as we held each other tightly.

*His goodness and love for me shone through, but I couldn't help being scared.*

❖ ❖ ❖

We found Elizabeth's experience so interesting that we called her to ask how it has affected her life since that time. Here is what she told us.

❖ ❖ ❖

Following this experience with the angel there was a lot more peace between my sister and me. We both decided to work out our disagreements more kindly. I can't truthfully say that I've always been successful in this effort. But even now, more than five years later, I find it much easier to remember that Jesus really does want me to be good, and to reach out to Him for His love to be in my heart.

Also, when I have conflicts with anyone, I try to work things out peaceably, and not react too quickly. I try to make peace, even when I'm not at fault. Not that I wish to pretend I'm perfect. I have my faults and struggles. But I also know I have God's help to overcome and to become more and more like Jesus, who sent the angel to alert me to my serious temper problem and help me throughout life to gain the victory.

Elizabeth's amazing account of her angel experience calls to mind Jesus' beatitude: "Blessed are the peacemakers, For they shall be called sons of God" (Matthew 5:9). Paul exhorted believers, "Follow peace with all men, and holiness, without which no man shall see the Lord: Looking diligently lest any man fail of the grace of God; lest any root of bitterness springing up trouble you, and thereby many be defiled" (Hebrews 12:14, KJV).

# Angel in the Snow

Gaston Paulin, a French Canadian, who pastors a church in Tennessee, tells of a memorable incident in his childhood that illustrates the importance of listening to our angel when he prompts us with a message of warning. Gaston writes:

In my childhood home we had a copy of a large painting that depicted a guardian angel tenderly watching over a sleeping baby. My belief in angels was as constant as the presence of the beautiful picture in the wall. But not until one fateful winter morning did I believe that my angel was always present to protect and guide me. It happened in my hometown of Quebec when I was ten or eleven years old.

A few weeks before I had received a bright red toy shovel as a Christmas present. Eager for the opportunity to use it, I waited for snow. Every day after Christmas I sprang out of bed and ran to the window to see if it had snowed. Finally one night it came. Throughout the night big fluffy flakes had blanketed the stark landscape, transforming it into a world of pure and dazzling white. In the morning, after gazing out the window wide-eyed for a few moments, I raced downstairs to our living room, where the shovel lay waiting under the Christmas tree. I grabbed my shovel and, though still in my pajamas, started to put on my snow boots. My mother stopped me and insisted that I have breakfast and get fully dressed before rushing out to play. Never did a boy so hastily gulp down his food or put on his winter wear.

Soon I was outside and reveling in the snow. A huge snowplow had passed along our street earlier leaving a high bank of snow in front of our driveway. It was perfect for digging a tunnel. Feverishly I set to work with my red shovel and soon hollowed out a space into which I could walk. It was so quiet and still inside my hand-dug cave, and I was so tired from all the exertion that without thinking about it I curled up, clutching my shovel, and fell asleep in my snug little retreat.

Totally oblivious to where I was, I began to dream. But breaking in on my heavy slumbers I heard a voice urgently say, "Gaston, wake up and get out!" Startled at first, I looked around but could see no one and hear nothing. Vaguely aware that I was still in my snow cave, I drifted off to sleep again. I do not know how many minutes passed before I heard the voice again, only this time more urgent and imperative, "Gaston, wake up, and get out, now!"

The voice awakened me like an electric shock. Forgetting everything else, I quickly scurried out of my little grotto. Moments later I saw a huge ice-grinding vehicle and dump truck move parallel up our street. The grinder was rapidly consuming the snow bank, funneling it into the truck.

Then it struck me—no one in my house or on the street knew where I had been. The voice must have been that of my angel. If he had not jarred me awake by his urgent command I would have been ground up with the snow and would have sprung awake too late to escape this gruesome end. How thankful I was for my angel who kept watch over me while I slept, and alerted me to my danger at the crucial moment.

Ever since then have I never doubted the reality of guardian angels. This incident occurred more than forty years ago, but throughout my life I have been positively affected by this experience. I have tried to make it a practice to seek God's guidance in all my activities, so that I might live to His glory. I look forward to thanking my angel face to face someday for his loving vigilance over me, and learning from him the innumerable other circumstances where he protected and guided me in harmony with my Savior's will and purpose of my life.

# The Man Who Wouldn't Hang

As we have seen repeatedly in the stories in this book, the miraculous intervention of angels has not been limited to Bible times. And one of the angels' main functions is to operate as ministers of God's justice. After all, they delight in upholding God's righteous law. That is why the Psalmist declared, "Bless the Lord, ye his angels, that excel in strength, that do his commandments, hearkening unto the voice of his word" (Psalm 103:20, KJV). They love to vindicate the innocent, and often intervene in mysterious, unexpected ways to do so.

When H. M. J. Richards was a young boy in Exeter, England, he witnessed a remarkable event that impressed itself on the public mind for many years. Robert E. Edwards tells the story.

A young man named John Lee was accused and convicted of murder. Though he persistently maintained his innocence, he was sentenced to hang.

The night before his execution, young John Lee had a dream. He saw himself being led out of his cell and through the prison corridor to the gallows. There he ascended the thirteen steps to the platform. A guard blindfolded him and placed the noose around his neck. After Lee said his last words, the executioner pulled the lever to spring the trap door, but nothing happened. Then John Lee woke up.

The following morning, young H. M. J. Richards joined with most of Exeter's population as they stood around the prison, waiting to see the flag go up in the prison courtyard at the appointed moment to signal the accomplishment of the execution. They waited in vain, for the flag never appeared. John Lee's dream had proven true. It all went just as he had seen in his sleep. The trap door refused to function.

After their unsuccessful attempt, the guards led the prisoner from the scaffold, then carefully checked and oiled the simple machinery that operated the trap door. Placing a bag of sand on the trap door, they pulled the lever, and saw the bag drop to the pavement below. Again they placed Lee over the trap door, adjusted the noose over his neck, and pulled the lever with decisive force. But the trap stayed firmly locked in place.

With grim consternation the guards conducted Lee off the platform again and retested their equipment, only to find it in perfect working order. For the third time they led their submissive prisoner to the place of his scheduled execution. Making sure that the noose was snug and that he stood squarely on the middle of the trap door, they jerked the lever again. But the gallows refused to drop Lee to his judicially ordered death.

*Again they adjusted the noose around his neck and pulled the lever with decisive force.*

Shaken by this turn of events, the warden telegraphed Queen Victoria with the baffling news. She ordered Lee's sentence to be commuted to life imprisonment, since they had not been able to execute him after three tries. Years later, the authorities freed John Lee when someone finally confessed to the crime for which Lee had been unjustly condemned.

Who held up the trap door that was supposed to hurtle Lee to his dreadful end? Surely it was an angel, sent by the Lord to protect an innocent man.

## The Man Who Wouldn't Hang

Jesus, the ultimate innocent Man, refused to summon an angel guard when He was being subjected to injustice. His disciple Peter erupted with indignation at the moment of Jesus' arrest, however. Peter unsheathed his sword and swung out wildly, and he succeeded in severing the ear of Malchus, the servant of Israel's high priest. Lightly freeing his hands from His captors, Jesus reached out and healed Malchus's wounded ear and, turning to Peter, said, "Put your sword back into its place, for all who take the sword will perish by the sword. Or do you think that I cannot now pray to My Father, and He will provide Me with more than twelve legions of angels? How then could the Scriptures be fulfilled, that it must happen thus?" (Matthew 26:52-54). By His very statement that He could have called legions of angels to His side at that fateful hour Jesus was bringing to our attention how closely angels monitor the affairs on earth, and how keenly they are poised to uphold justice.

# Angels at War in Heaven

Angels are no strangers to war. As incongruous as it sounds, the first war ever fought was by angels in heaven. John writes in the book of Revelation, "War broke out in heaven: Michael and his angels fought against the dragon; and the dragon and his angels fought, but they did not prevail, nor was a place found for them in heaven any longer" (Revelation 12:7, 8).

How did heaven become the first battlefield? It all began with Lucifer, the highest-ranking angel who defected because of pride over his vast abilities and power. Ezekiel 28 and Isaiah 14 tell the story. Egotism, power hunger, jealousy over his subordination to the Godhead and especially to Jesus, the co-creator of the Universe with His Father and the Holy Spirit—all these factors combined to promote rebellion in Lucifer's heart.

It did not have to be that way. Physically and mentally, Lucifer was created perfect. God gave Him a flawless education. Heaven's laws were reasonable then as they are now. Living conditions were perfect—no poverty, sickness, disease, inequity, no harsh rule, unreasonable requirements, or arbitrary exercise of power on God's part. But one thing God would not do was to create His intelligent beings to give Him preprogrammed loyalty and praise.

Instead He endowed angels and other cosmic intelligent beings with innate powers to grow mentally and morally and to exercise freedom of choice. True, all were created to harmonize naturally with God's character and will, but this inborn bent to obey was to be sustained voluntarily by each being, rather than maintained by coercion. Plainly put, any being at any time could choose to disobey God, and strike out on a path of independence. Never would God give any provocation to that, not even by being uncommunicative about the goodness of His ways and laws. God has always been generously self-revealing, always willing to communicate with His creatures.

When Lucifer rebelled, God did not leave him or the angels in the dark about the terrible results that would follow from his departure from the right way. Lucifer had launched an elaborate campaign to misrepresent God to the angels. One can readily deduce from his brash rantings recorded in Isaiah 14 that his complaints included allegations of tyranny on God's part, unfairness in His law, and suppression of personal liberty. The fact that he was able to ensnare a third of the angels, who all knew what God is really like, should warn us that Satan's powers of deception are very great. It should also convince us that we need to fully trust God and submit to His grace and authority if we want to be rescued from the horrible effects of sin and rebellion.

Scripture tells us that God does not change. Therefore we can safely assume that prior to open warfare in heaven, God did everything within the reach of His infinite love and wisdom to call Lucifer back from his subversive alienation. The loyal angels undoubtedly did all they could to dissuade Lucifer and his angel followers from their growing moral madness. Each angel was free to choose masters—Lucifer or Christ. Lucifer's defiance mounted; his charges grew more strident and desperate. He forced a showdown. Then war erupted in heaven. The arch-rebel

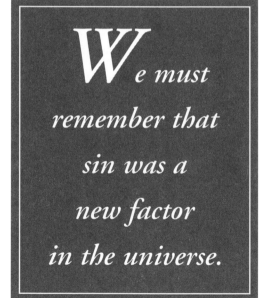

*We must remember that sin was a new factor in the universe.*

and his followers were cast out.

We might ask, why didn't God simply destroy Satan, once his hostility to truth and love became so apparent? We must remember that sin was a new factor in the universe. Not even the loyal angels could fully conceive of its final effects. And since God's trustworthiness had been called into question by Satan, the Lord deemed it wisest to allow this adversary to act out his plans in full so that everyone could trace the course of sin from its seemingly innocuous beginnings to its truly devastating end. That is why Paul identified this planet as the theater of the universe, viewed by angels and men (see 1 Corinthians 4:9). By seeing Satan fully exhibit his character and purposes, all could see beyond question that no justification can be found for disobedience to God, and no good results can come of it. Thus the universe is rendered sin-proof.

# CHAPTER
# 23

# Sheltered in a Church

At Darventa, Serbia in 1992, Philip and a band of six teenagers were pinned down under the crossfire of opposing armies. Philip and his friends belonged to no faction. They only wished for peace in their land. But now they were in desperate need of shelter—anywhere free from the relentless shelling and bombing that threatened to destroy the whole town.

Crawling along the besieged hillside, Philip and his friends headed to a bombed-out building that offered at least the protection of a ragged portion of roof, brick walls, and a few battered rooms whose masonry hadn't yet collapsed. Night had fallen, and the young men began exploring the layout of their new shelter. Soon they discovered a large room with chairs lined up in rows facing a slightly elevated platform. Being Muslims and unfamiliar with Christian meeting places, it took them a while to discover that they were in a Protestant church. This place was their shelter for the next two months.

One of the least damaged rooms had books and pictures for children. Eventually the boys concluded that this was a place of worship, and they chose to treat it with reverence. Sensing that the pulpit and organ were connected with sacred service, the boys always kept back from that area. A small closet-like space near the front door was nearly intact. Accordingly, the boys selected it as a post for sentry duty, which they shared on a rotating schedule. Around the walls of this little room were shelves stacked with books, some of which were scarred from bullets.

Finding a Bible in the collection, Philip began to read but got bogged down after the first three chapters of Genesis. Spotting a book entitled *The Great Controversy*, Philip became curious and pulled it from the shelf. The very name of the book seemed pertinent to the circumstances they were in. Galvanized by the prophetic message of this book that described world conditions with which he was all too familiar, Philip read through the book. When he returned the book to the shelf, Philip noticed the address of the publishing house in Belgrade. Because of the unusual street name given, this address stayed in his memory.

From time to time the boys had to venture forth from their battered shelter to find food and water. Unable to use the door because it was vulnerable to sniper fire, Philip had to crawl through a side window frame, above which hung a picture of Christ with outstretched hands and the inscription "Come Unto Me." This picture and its invitation irritated Philip. "How can I believe in a God of mercy and love in this violence-racked world, where I could be cut down by bullets any moment, day after day?"

Then came his turn to search for supplies. Just as he was about to climb out the window, Philip heard an unfamiliar voice call his name aloud directly behind him. Stepping back quickly from the window, he turned around to look for the caller but saw no one. At that moment a volley of gunfire shattered the window frame and pocked the walls. Without recognizing its identity, Philip had just been rescued by his guardian angel from being shot. But it was clear to him and his companions that they had been discovered. Flight was now imperative.

Sensing that a divine call had been in the voice that warned him from going through the window, Philip prayed for a lull in the shelling so that he and his companions could make their way to safety. No sooner had he prayed than the shelling stopped. Seizing the moment, Philip shouted to his companions, "This is a sign. It's time for us to escape now." Clambering out the window, they all raced down the hillside into the shattered city, while the gunfire following them from behind fell short of its mark.

Several months later the war ended. Tired, dispirited, and emaciated, Philip decided to try contacting his sister Suada, who had escaped from their town about a year earlier to live with their grandparents in another city. But she was not there. A thin trail of leads finally placed in his possession the telephone number of a school near the city of Marusavec, where someone thought she might be staying as a refugee.

To his joy, Philip reached Suada by phone, and learned from her that she was very happy in her new location. "This place is too nice for me to describe to you over the phone. You must come and see it for yourself," she told him.

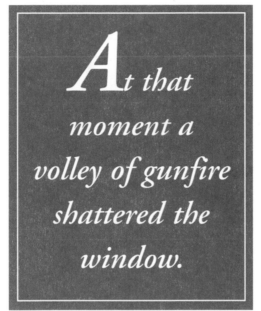

*At that moment a volley of gunfire shattered the window.*

Philip received a very cordial welcome from the people at the school where Suada was enrolled as a student. Never had he seen her so happy before. Suada shared with Philip some of the books she was reading at the school. To his astonishment he saw on the flyleaf of the book the same address in Belgrade that he had seen in so many of the bullet-ridden books on the shelves of his hiding place in Darventa. Now he felt impelled to study the literature and religion that had come to mean so much to his beloved sister. He enrolled for the next semester at this school. As a college graduate in electrical engineering, he had little difficulty in catching up with all the studies. Biblical Greek and theology were new to this young Muslim man, but he proved an apt student, and found himself drawn to the Christian faith.

Later, during a visit to a church in Zagreb he met a young woman by the name of Blanka. After they got to know each other, love blossomed between them. In 1994 Philip was baptized, and he also married Blanka. He and Blanka have gone back to Darventa, where they are now working to rebuild and restore the bombed-out church that was once his shelter. It is now Philip's ambition to help people find refuge, not from bombs and bullets, but from sin, by taking refuge in the Savior, Jesus, whose angel rescued him and has protected him through his beleaguered odyssey to redemption.—Adapted from an article by Don Jacobson, *Adventist Review*, January 1999.

# CHAPTER
## 24

# Angels in the Hereafter

Scripture tells us that sights, sounds, and experiences far beyond human powers of description and imagination await the redeemed. "Eye has not seen, nor ear heard, Nor have entered into the heart of man The things which God has prepared for those who love Him" (1 Corinthians 2:9). Our limited, earth-bound senses make it impossible for us to more than dimly grasp the boundless glories beyond this age.

In the hereafter, all that was lost by sin will be restored. Right now our world trembles with the wounds of war, the defacement of nature through human exploitation and carelessness, and the ravages of earthquake, fire, flood, and storm. And the most unsettling force of all is human injustice—prejudice, bigotry, and violence. All these hostile forces have made our world a place of pain and woe.

But it was not always so. When the world was young, God pronounced it very good (see Genesis 1:31). It was His Creation, the product of His perfect mind and power. But sin, brought on by Satan, and embraced by our first parents, disrupted the perfection of God's original order and thrust desolation into the very heart of human experience. Humanity embarked on a strange alliance with Satan. But the whole Bible from beginning to end tells us of God's plan to uproot the power and presence of sin from the universe through His plan of salvation. God's angels have been deeply involved in this plan from its start, and will continue to be involved till the day of final victory.

That is why one of our chief delights in future glory will be our friendship with these heavenly helpers. In vision, Zechariah heard God promise Joshua, Israel's high priest, who represents all redeemed people, "If you will walk in My ways, And if you will keep My command, . . . I will give you places to walk among these who stand here" (Zechariah 3:7).

Because this scene was set in God's sanctuary, His operational headquarters, we can readily determine that the ones standing by were the angels who serve God day and night in His presence, and run divinely appointed errands between heaven and earth for our benefit.

This special face-to-face fellowship with angels will begin the very day of Christ's return. Jesus will send forth His heavenly messengers to greet the redeemed whom He awakens from the grave and glorifies with the living saints. Imagine the thrill of rising through the air with these winged friends who so often have cheered us in our lonely hours, braced us in times of trial, protected us in times of danger, comforted us in times of bereavement, and instructed us in our days of searching and doubt. We will not lack for subjects of discussion as we travel to heaven with these angels. And the greatest subject of all in our conversation with them will be the mysteries and marvels of our Savior's love as revealed in the plan of salvation. It is this theme that grips the interest of the angels (see 1 Peter 1:10-12). Throughout eternity, redeemed humanity and the angels who have had so much to do with drawing us to the Savior and keeping us close to Him, will marvel and glory over the plan of salvation. (See Revelation 5:11-14; 7:9-15.)

Throughout their ministry for us on earth angels have been communicators of God's truth. No doubt they will continue in that capacity in heaven and on the earth made new. With the veil parted between the past, present, and future we will be able to clearly see how, with skill and love, the angels worked behind the scenes of our lives every day to bring us to God and guide us into understanding and doing His will. Every rustle of their wings and every whisper of their voices declares His glory and conveys the music of divine love. Every influence and interposition of angels working on our behalf is directed to magnify the cross of Jesus and illuminate our hearts with the boundless glories of perfect love.

Through Satan's crafty deceptions, heaven was depopulated of one-third of the angels. Imagine the loyal angels' grief over their lost and rebellious companions who once loved the Lord and delighted in serving Him. Their grief is assuaged at the thought that the vacancies left in heaven by their former companions will be filled by the earth's redeemed millions, transformed from rebels to eternally loyal and grateful subjects of God's kingdom.

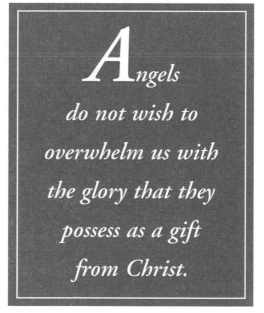

*Angels do not wish to overwhelm us with the glory that they possess as a gift from Christ.*

Today the angels hide their names from us and keep their identity muted. They do not wish to overwhelm us with the glory that they possess as a gift from Christ. In the hereafter we will know their names and be charmed by the striking individuality of each noble, selfless servant of God. But we shall never make the mistake of worshiping them or letting our admiration for them eclipse our love for Jesus.

Heaven's greatest light will not flash from angels' wings nor glint from crowns of victory the saints will wear, but will shine from the places where Christ bore the wounds of Calvary for us. Habakkuk, seeing Christ in a heavenly vision of future glory, records, "He has rays flashing from His hand, And there is the hiding of His power" (Habakkuk 3:4, NASB). It is the power of love, the power of grace, the power of mercy that Satan's darkest waves of rage were powerless to quench. For God's love is stronger than death and the grave, mightier than any foe who would stand between our souls and the Savior.

For this reason the science of redemption is the greatest of all sciences. The redeemed, the unfallen angels, and worlds that never sinned will join together in studying the inexhaustible theme of God's self-sacrificing love, as displayed on Calvary, and in all heaven's benevolent deeds on behalf of fallen humanity. The

hearts of all the ransomed will thrill with ever-expanding devotion to the Lamb. To heaven's angels, the reward for their labors over the past six thousand years will be the satisfaction of having worked in effective partnership with God for the salvation of human beings who will now be their companions for all eternity.

Stacey C. a teenager from Wichita, Kansas, said it well: "One main thing I look forward to in heaven is the joy of meeting my angel and thanking him for all his hard work in leading me to Christ. Right now I just want to learn how to listen to my angel and to the Holy Spirit, so that I can do God's will and help others the way I should. I don't want all of God's unselfish work for me to go to waste." That's a good philosophy of life, isn't it? One to which all the angels of heaven can join their voices in saying, "Amen!"

C H A P T E R
# 25

# Who Are the Angels: What Does the Bible Say?

So many theories exist regarding the identity, origin, and activity of angels. The truth about angels is far more beautiful than the best of human imagination could create. So, let's see what the Bible has to say about angels.

## Origin

### Angels are divine beings created by Christ.

"Praise him, all his angels, praise him all his heavenly hosts. . . . Let them praise the name of the Lord, for he commanded and they were created" (Psalm 148:2, 5, NIV, see also Colossians 1:16).

### They are not self-existent or self-sustaining, but derive all their power and life from Christ.

"In the past God spoke to our forefathers through the prophets at many times and in various ways, but in these last days he has spoken to us by his Son, whom he appointed heir of all things, and through whom he made the universe. The Son is the radiance of God's glory . . . So he became as much superior to the angels as the name he has inherited is superior to theirs" (Hebrews 1:1-4, NIV).

### *They existed before the creation of our world and humanity.*

" 'Where were you when I laid the earth's foundation? Tell me, if you understand. Who marked off its dimensions? Surely you know! Who stretched a measuring line across it? On what were its footings set, or who laid its cornerstone—while the morning stars sang together and all the angels shouted for joy?' " (Job 38:4-7, NIV; see also Genesis 3:24).

## Nature

### *They are spirits subject to God's authority.*

"In speaking of the angels he says, 'He makes his angels winds, his servants flames of fire.' . . . Are not all angels ministering spirits sent to serve those who will inherit salvation?" (Hebrews 1:7, 14, NIV; see also 1 Peter 3:22).

### *They are not human beings, but are of a higher order.*

" 'What is man that you are mindful of him, the son of man that you care for him? You made him a little lower than the angels; you crowned him with glory and honor' " (Hebrews 2:6, 7, NIV; see also Psalm 8:4, 5).

### *Their nature differs from ours.*

"Since the children have flesh and blood, he [Jesus] too shared in their humanity so that by his death he might . . . free those who all their lives were held in slavery by their fear of death. For surely it is not angels he helps, but Abraham's descendants" (Hebrews 2:14-16, NIV).

## Who Are the Angels?

***They are mighty, powerful, glorious beings.***

"This will happen when the Lord Jesus is revealed from heaven in blazing fire with his powerful angels" (2 Thessalonians 1:7, NIV; see also Psalm 104:4).

***Angels obey God's commandments.***

"Praise the Lord, you his angels, you mighty ones who do his bidding, who obey his word" (Psalm 103:20, NIV).

***Like human beings, they have freedom of choice to obey or disobey God.***

"And the angels who did not keep their positions of authority but abandoned their own home—these he has kept in darkness, bound with everlasting chains for judgment on the great Day" (Jude 6, NIV).

***They can travel between heaven and earth infinitely faster than the speed of light.***

"While I was still in prayer, Gabriel, the man I had seen in the earlier vision, came to me in swift flight about the time of the evening sacrifice. He . . . said to me, . . . 'As soon as you began to pray, an answer was given, which I have come to tell you' " (Daniel 9:21-23, NIV; see also John 1:51).

***Human beings do not become heavenly angels at death or under any circumstances.***

" 'Those who are considered worthy of taking part in that age and in the resurrection from the dead . . . can no longer die; for they are *like* the angels. They are God's children, since they are children of the resurrection' " (Luke 20:35, 36, NIV, emphasis supplied).

*In their work on earth angels sometimes appear as human beings.*

"As they entered the tomb, they saw a young man dressed in a white robe sitting on the right side, and they were alarmed" (Mark 16:5, NIV; compare Matthew 28:2-5 where this person is called "an angel of the Lord"; see also Genesis 19:1-11; Hebrews 13:2).

*There are different orders of angels: seraphim, cherubim, and other unspecified orders.*

"Above him [God] were seraphs, each with six wings" (Isaiah 6:2, NIV). "After he [God] drove the man out, he placed on the east side of the Garden of Eden cherubim and a flaming sword flashing back and forth to guard the way to the tree of life" (Genesis 3:24, NIV). "Then I looked and heard the voice of many angels, numbering thousands upon thousands, and ten thousand times ten thousand. They encircled the throne" (Revelation 5:11, NIV).

*Their supreme commander is Michael, the archangel.*

"And their was war in heaven. Michael and his angels fought against the dragon, and the dragon and his angels fought back" (Revelation 12:7, NIV).

## Population and Habitat

*Their home is in heaven—specifically, God's sanctuary.*

"The Lord reigns, let the nations tremble; he sits enthroned between the cherubim" (Psalm 99:1, NIV; see also Isaiah 6:1-4).

*They stand in God's presence and have direct access to Him at all times.*

"The angel answered, 'I am Gabriel. I stand in the presence of God' "(Luke

1:19, NIV).   " 'See that you do not look down on one of these little ones. For I tell you that their angels in heaven always see the face of my Father in heaven' " (Matthew 18:10, NIV).

***They are dispatched to all parts of the universe, particularly to our world.***

" 'You shall see heaven open, and the angels of God ascending and descending on the Son of Man' " (John 1:51, NIV; see also Psalm 68:17).

***Angels are innumerable.***

"You have come to thousands upon thousands of angels in joyful assembly" (Hebrews 12:22, NIV; see also Daniel 7:10).

## Work and Interests

***Heaven's angels are deeply interested in our salvation and the means of its accomplishment through Christ.***

"Concerning this salvation, the prophets . . . searched intently and with the greatest care, trying to find out the time and circumstances to which the Spirit of Christ in them was pointing when he predicted the sufferings of Christ and the glories that would follow. . . . Even angels long to look into these things" (1 Peter 1:10-12, NIV; see also Luke 15:10).

***Angels are God's messengers.***

"Praise the Lord, you his angels, you mighty ones who do his bidding, who obey his word" (Psalm 103:20, NIV).

***Angels know our names, addresses, and occupations.***

"One day at about three in the afternoon he [Cornelius] had a vision. He distinctly saw an angel of God, who came to him and said, 'Cornelius!' Cornelius stared at him in fear. 'What is it, Lord?' he asked. The angel answered, . . . 'Send men to Joppa to bring back a man named Simon who is called Peter. He is staying with Simon the tanner, whose house is by the sea.' " (Acts 10:3-6, NIV)

### Angels give instruction to God's people.

"A certain man of Zorah, named Manoah, from the clan of the Danites, had a wife who was sterile and remained childless. The angel of the Lord appear to her and said, 'You are sterile and childless, but you are going to conceive and have a son. Now see to it that you drink no wine or other fermented drink and that you do not eat anything unclean, because you will conceive and give birth to a son. No razor may be used on his head, because the boy is to be a Nazirite, set apart to God from birth, and he will begin the deliverance of Israel from the hands of the Philistines' "(Judges 13:2-5, NIV; see also Acts 7:53).

### Angels are deeply involved with helping God's people preach the gospel.

"Then the high priest and all his associates, who were members of the party of the Sadducees, were filled with jealousy. They arrested the apostles and put them in the public jail. But during the night an angel of the Lord opened the doors of the jail and brought them out. 'Go, stand in the temple courts,' he said, 'and tell the people the full message of this new life' "(Acts 5:17-20, NIV; see also Revelation 14:6).

### God uses angels as ministers of justice.

"I saw in heaven another great and marvelous sign: seven angels with the seven last plagues—last, because with them God's wrath is completed" (Revelation 15:1, NIV; see also Numbers 22:22-35; 2 Kings 19:35; Daniel 4:14-17, 31-33; Revelation 16).

## Who Are the Angels?

**Angels guide, direct, protect, and provide for God's servants.**

"The angel of the Lord encamps around those who fear him, and he delivers them" (Psalm 34:7, NIV; see also 1 Kings 19:5-7; 2 Kings 1:3, 15; Psalm 91:11; Acts 27:23).

**Angels intervene in world affairs, holding back destructive forces, restraining tyrants, and punishing evil.**

"After this I saw four angels standing at the four corners of the earth, holding back the four winds of the earth to prevent any wind from blowing on the land or on the sea or on any tree. Then I saw another angel coming up from the east, having the seal of the living God. He called out in a loud voice to the four angels who had been given power to harm the land and the sea: 'Do not harm the land or the sea or the trees until we put a seal on the foreheads of the servants of our God' "(Revelation 7:1-3, NIV; see also Daniel 10:10-14; Acts 12:20-24).

**Each person has a guardian angel.**

" 'See that you do not look down on one of these little ones. For I tell you that their angels in heaven always see the face of my Father in heaven' " (Matthew 18:10, NIV).

**Angels are witnesses in God's work of judgment.**

" ' "Thrones were set in place, and the Ancient of Days took his seat. His clothing was as white as snow; the hair of his head was white like wool. His throne was flaming with fire, and its wheels were all ablaze. A river of fire was flowing, coming out from before him. Thousands upon thousands attended him; ten thousand times ten thousand stood before him. The court was seated, and the books were opened" ' " (Daniel 7:9-10, NIV; see also Revelation 5:8-14).

**Angels refuse to be worshiped, but they worship God.**

"I, John, am the one who heard and saw these things. And when I had heard and seen them, I fell down to worship at the feet of the angel who had been showing them to me. But he said to me, 'Do not do it! I am a fellow servant with you and with your brothers the prophets and of all who keep the words of this book. Worship God!' " (Revelation 22:8, 9, NIV; see also 19:10; Hebrews 1:6).

**Angels will all accompany Christ at His return and gather the redeemed from all parts of the earth, separating the wicked from the righteous.**

" 'They will see the Son of Man coming on the clouds of the sky, with power and great glory. And he will send his angels with a loud trumpet call, and they will gather his elect from the four winds, from one end of the heavens to the other' " (Matthew 24:30, 31, NIV; see also 13:39, 49).

# Evil Angels:
# What Does the Bible Say?

### Origin of Evil Angels

*Lucifer, an exalted and perfect angel in heaven, chose to sin and rebel against God. As a result, He became Satan and was banished to this earth.*

" ' "You were the model of perfection, full of wisdom and perfect in beauty. . . . You were anointed as a guardian cherub, for so I ordained you. You were on the holy mount of God; . . . You were blameless in your ways from the day you were created till wickedness was found in you. . . . So I drove you in disgrace from the mount of God, and I expelled you O guardian cherub, . . . Your heart became proud on account of your beauty, and you corrupted your wisdom because of your splendor. So I threw you to the earth" ' " (Ezekiel 28:12, 14-17, NIV).

"How have you fallen from heaven, O morning star, son of the dawn! You have been cast down to the earth, . . . You said in your heart, 'I will ascend to heaven; I will raise my throne above the stars of God; . . . I will make myself like the Most High' " (Isaiah 14:12-14, NIV).

***Sin, murder, and lying originated with Satan.***

"He who does what is sinful is of the devil, because the devil has been sinning from the beginning" (1 John 3:8, NIV).

" 'You belong to your father the devil, . . . He was a murderer from the beginning, not holding to the truth, for there is no truth in him. When he lies, he speaks his native language, for he is a liar and the father of lies' " (John 8:44, NIV).

***One third of the good angels in heaven joined Lucifer's rebellion. They were banished to earth with him and no longer have access to heaven.***

"Then another sign appeared in heaven: an enormous red dragon. . . . His tail swept a third of the stars out of the sky and flung them to the earth. . . . The great dragon was hurled down—that ancient serpent called the devil or Satan, who leads the whole world astray. He was hurled to the earth, and his angels with him" (Revelation 12:3, 4, 9, NIV; see also Jude 6; 2 Peter 2:4).

## Work and Purposes

***The chief occupation of Satan and his angels is to tempt men and women to rebel against God by disobeying Him and His commandments.***

"Be self-controlled and alert. Your enemy the devil prowls around like a roaring lion looking for someone to devour" (1 Peter 5:8, NIV).

"And he [Jesus] was in the desert forty days, being tempted by Satan" (Mark 1:13, NIV).

***God's people are to resist the devil and his angels by God's grace.***

"Be strong in the Lord and in his mighty power. Put on the full armor of God so that you can take your stand against the devil's schemes. For our struggle is not against flesh and blood, but against . . . the powers of this dark world and against the spiritual forces of evil in the heavenly realms" (Ephesians 6:10-12, NIV).

"Resist the devil, and he will flee from you. Come near to God, and he will come near to you" (James 4:7,8, NIV).

***Satan and his angels will work even harder as the second coming of Jesus draws near.***

" 'Woe to the earth and the sea, because the devil has gone down to you! He is filled with fury, because he knows that his time is short' " (Revelation 12:12, NIV).

"The Spirit clearly says that in later times some will abandon the faith and follow deceiving  spirits and things taught by demons" (1 Timothy 4:1, NIV).

## The Future Fate of Evil Angels

***Satan and his angels are reserved by God for eventual judgment.***

"God did not spare angels when they sinned, but sent them . . . to be held for judgment" (2 Peter 2:4, NIV).

***Satan and his angels will be destroyed by fire, never to exist again.***

" 'Then he [God] will say to those on his left, "Depart from me, you who are cursed, into the eternal fire prepared for the devil and his angels" ' " (Matthew 25:41, NIV).

## Great Stories for Kids

Your children will love the adventures and drama of the five-volume set *Great Stories for Kids*, and you'll value the character-building lessons they learn while reading these treasured stories. Each volume is bound in durable hardcover with delightful color illustrations. Also available in Spanish and French.

## The Bible Story

*The Bible Story* was written not just to tell the wonderful stories in the Bible, but each story was especially written to teach your child a different character-building lesson—lessons such as honesty, respect for parents, obedience, kindness, and many more. This is truly the pleasant way to influence your child's character. The set contains more than 400 stories spread over 10 volumes. Hardcover.

## My Bible Friends

Imagine your child's delight as you read the charming story of Small Donkey, who carried tired Mary up the hill toward Bethlehem. Or of Zacchaeus the Cheater, who climbed a sycamore tree so he could see Jesus passing by. Each book has four attention-holding stories written in simple, crystal-clear language. And the colorful illustrations surpass in quality what you may have seen in any other children's Bible story book. Five volumes, hardcover. Also available in videos and audio cassettes.

## Desire of Ages

This is E. G. White's monumental bestseller on the life of Christ. It is perhaps the most spiritually perceptive of the Savior's biographies since The Gospel According to John. Here Jesus becomes more than a historic figure—he is the great divine-human personality set forth in a hostile world to make peace between God and man. Two volumes, hardcover.

**For more information, mail the postpaid card, or write to:**
**Pacific Press Marketing Service, P.O. Box 5353, Nampa, ID 83653.**